Tending the Fire

Poetry for the Emerging Sage

Poems by
Marilyn Loy Every, DMin

For publishing inquiries:
Sapient Publishing
www.Sagessence.com

ISBN: 978-0-9910354-2-7

Library of Congress Data on File with the Publisher

Printed in the USA

10 9 8 7 6 5 4 3 2

Tending the Fire

IS DEDICATED TO

Kristen, my daughter,
and
Matthew, my son,
my champions
and sources of my fire
to be a worthy sage

Accolades from Admired Sages

"With graceful and artistic expression, Marilyn Loy Every courageously engages readers at the heart level through her sacred, mesmeric poetry. She is a prolific visionary for the sage archetype emerging in our culture, and a creative guide in manifesting vibrant possibilities for vital, conscious aging. Her poems connect issues of aging with raw hope and fresh perspective, ultimately gifting us with our own wise reflections. *Tending the Fire* prompts deep musings relative to envisioning our precious lives well-lived—each poem truly a priceless gift!"

—Joan Borysenko, PhD
New York Times best-selling author of
Minding the Body, Mending the Mind

"Marilyn Loy Every stimulates the imagination with richly-textured, vibrant and beautiful metaphors and images, inviting one to move beyond words to be open to the grand birthing of wisdom in the sageing years of our lives. Her splendid poetry, engaging so profoundly in Gaia, stimulates one not to look to others to be sages, but to awaken to the sageing happening in our hearts, minds and souls. She guides us with insight and strength through the process of claiming our sageing. Doing so she encourages us to offer to our families, communities and society the full experience of the wisdom we have to share. Her poetry is a magnificent gift to the reader, personally, and to the larger community of which the reader is a part. *Tending the Fire* is a deeply satisfying, engaging body of work by one who has made the journey to, and in being, a sage."

—J. Melvin Bricker, DMin
Board Member Creation Spirituality Communities
and The Fox Institute for Creation Spirituality.

"For both women and men, honoring elder years is now—more than ever before—imperative. Our culture historically reveres youth and unconsciously ignores the wisdom and resourceful potential gained by years of living. Marilyn Loy Every's poetry gives a bold voice and fearless insights for many who are hungry to behold aging from a spirited, life-giving stance."

—Rev. Dr. Lauren Artress
Founder, Veriditas and
the World-Wide Labyrinth Project

CONTENTS

Tending the Fire

ACKNOWLEDGMENTS

Tending the Fire

It is an honor to engage with so many wise people who share their inspiring life experiences, challenges, heart aches and joy—all of which significantly influence the themes and texture of my poetry. I had the privilege of spending many years in an audiology career whereby I met and worked mostly with individuals over the age of fifty. I extend my heartfelt gratitude to each whom openly shared from their heart situations and stories relative to their aging. Many became treasured friends who shined a light on re-envisioning a cultural aging paradigm.

There are two very influential people I want to acknowledge who always supported my vision in encouraging others to discern their life as a sage. Marvin Evans had a zest and reverence for life that was brilliant. Regardless of what life brought his way, Marvin responded with a sense of humor, and with uncanny wisdom in reframing circumstances. He always regarded life with welcome, awe and respect. He regarded his last months of life as *radiant twilight*. Second, my dear friend Eleanor Deines who, now at 103 years old, leads readings for groups using my poetry. She is a light in the world like no other. She is an exemplar as a sage, and is a lively inspiration that infuses my creative work. Eleanor's beauty and positive life philosophy illuminate the way of the sage for all who have the privilege of knowing her. Thank you, Eleanor, and thank you, Marvin, for being my priceless mentors.

I want to also acknowledge my parents and grandparents, who were my first mentors relative to aging. Even though they have left this life, I still learn from the positive choices they made, and from their attitudes, values and beliefs. They were dedicated to living their later years in authentic and affirming ways, no matter how difficult challenges were that they encountered.

I treasure the creative spirits of many others who have been and continue to be my mentors. They, who breathe with the potency and beauty of poetic expression, include my so-journeying poet friends, acclaimed poets, and wise women and men. Each is a treasure and always holds a cherished place in my heart. And, they continue to inspire me on my own path of sacred poetry.

INTRODUCTION

Tending the Fire

Many cultures celebrate the aging process and honor the elderly, while the Western culture continues to idealize youth and early life. In other traditions, men and women are esteemed as elders. Respect for elders is central to the family, and such positions are acclaimed and viewed as essential for the community. Their attitudes and practices have an incredibly positive effect on the process of aging. Wisdom gained from age is honored as a valuable resource.

Our society continues to focus on a youthful culture, yet the number of older Americans continues to increase. It is essential that we—as women and men who are daughters and sons, sisters and brothers, mothers and fathers, aunts and uncles, wives and husbands, teachers, business people, caregivers, and leaders—recognize and acknowledge the vast wisdom we have gained from decades of living. We have valuable and diverse life experiences. Thus, we have a wealth of creativity to offer our families, communities and our global neighbors. It is clear that now is a time for us in the second half of our lives to envision a new paradigm to achieve meaningful fulfillment in years to come.

Many older individuals in our Western culture are beginning to challenge what has previously been the socially accepted aging paradigm. Transformation that we hope for will emerge from a new life-affirming vision that includes liberating images, practices and lifestyles in creating a supportive model. Unless we reframe our personal views of aging, and live into a meaningful archetype, we will deprive our families, communities and society of the full experience we have to offer. We can *choose* to consciously evolve as exemplars for our culture!

We may begin this journey by answering emerging questions leading us through an undefined terrain that may just prompt our own radical transformation. Are we willing to repeat a familiar societal script, and continue expectations that previous generations have accepted? How can we become living examples of personal authenticity? What choices can we make to live more passionately? In what ways can we foster compassion? Will we truly recognize that we are our own masters to create a model that serves a new life-affirming vision? How then will we live our second half of life to its fullest?

For insights into our own personal questions, we may be tempted to seek out the most reliable and knowledgeable sources. However, I propose awakening to our inner fire—our own source of wisdom—and tending to that fire consciously and diligently. Such wisdom from our *enlightened inner self* is a rich source for guidance. Deepening awareness of, and creating a relationship with, our unique and authentic wisdom can provide us with valuable personal leadership throughout all aspects of living into the second half of life.

Therefore, meaningful change begins within our own personal lives by connecting at a deeper level with our own wisdom and ability to create new views of ourselves. We are called to ignite our authentic potential to live even more dynamic and fulfilling lives beginning now. Integral to this process, of course, is for each of us to truly recognize and tend to that inner fire—our source of wisdom and immense wealth of creativity.

So, this is a time to take a deep look within. And, it is an essential time to name the *sage*, the wise one archetype. Metaphorically, our sage tends the cauldron of our wisdom and creativity where a flame fuels deeper authenticity, passion, compassion and inspiring vision for our life. Begin to imagine your sage as the enlightened inner self, and as your brilliant guiding light.

My hope is that throughout reading the poems in *Tending the Fire*, you will be inspired to begin to consciously integrate themes of authenticity, passion, compassion and inspiring vision in your own life. Messages in this poetry are intended to spark introspection that will take you deeper into your own discernment in tending to matters, issues, values and qualities that are most meaningful to you.

Poems relating to *The Sage Coming of Age* are truly an invitation to claim your own sage wisely guiding you through transitions of aging. We are on an unfolding journey of development, even through our death. Consciously recognizing and calling on our own unique wisdom is our profound foundation in daily adventures and endeavors.

As we begin to deepen in qualities of the sage, living authenticity becomes imperative.

The chapter *Flames of Authenticity* offers thoughts to ignite your genuine truth. As we live more authentically, we cannot help but expand our unique creative potential, and nurture our imagination to manifest ideas and dreams that may have been dormant for years. These are the flames that also inspire liberating images of aging.

The *Flames of Passion* invite us to live passionately in the moment, and to foster love, joy, wonder and gratitude. The poems are intended to encourage readers to become more open to discovery of expanded ways of deepening pleasures while living into elder years. They are also a call to thoughtfully and lovingly make life-affirming choices moment to moment.

As we move into our seasoned life, compassion becomes a vital, core strength. *Flames of Compassion* stir us to practice loving kindness, and to live into the flow of grief, loss and change. Compassion is essential as we accept more challenging opportunities to graciously give to others, as well as receive from others. And, compassion is crucial in order for us to live through our own life transitions confidently.

Flames of Vision call us to create living legacies that support greater good for our families, extending to the well-being of the planet. The poetry embodies provocation to manifest deeper fulfillment as we live each day. Reflections bid us to impart a wise, mentoring spirit for following generations, and encourage us to honor intergenerational connectedness.

Last, *Tending the Flames* poems are offerings for contemplating how we continue to honor ourselves as sages, and tend our cauldrons of great wisdom and creativity that are at our beck and call. As we awaken to the reality that we can claim the name of "sage" in our own right and in our chosen time, we can also be confident in our own unique wise sage leadership in whatever ways we envision.

Our small phase of time in this existence is precious. Our opportunities to leave our footprints are vast. As we come to the awesome realization that this is our moment, we can truly celebrate the liberating journey of aging. May each of us fully embrace the reality that we are the ones to tend to the powerful emergence of our own wise sage.

I encourage you to contemplatively hold each of the poems in *Tending the Fire* as a sacred reflection of life. I suggest exploring them from a perspective that takes you deeper into your own fire of discernment, inspiration and wisdom. May you enthusiastically tend to the fire in your heart urging you to bring about a new legacy as a creative sage in this new frontier. Welcome to the journey—*Tending the Fire*.

Tending the Fire

Poetry for the Emerging Sage

Vision of Sagessence

I come to you
to reveal a vision that
tumbles inside, condensed,
contained, living rib to rib.
Where shall be a next step?
Is it earth in our tread?
Or, an imprint yet to recede
into fresh, new, fertile soil?

Shall we rest in the settled dust
of culture's past knowing?
Or, lift our feet up
anticipating a daring turn?
Shall we tip toe to the edge
of society's comfort and gaze,
or collapse into arms
of Wisdom's sacred abyss?

Continue

Turning our ears to muffled,
distant heart sounds, implore,
"Please retell the story that
the Ancient Ones prophesied."
Then comes a deep whisper
rising through dense history,
You are a sage; and
I bid your holy consecration.

O fervent sages—
draw from your wells,
illuminate your Sagessence,
shine forth your sacred story.
Enliven the cosmic story!
The breath of god awaits
to bless what only you can live . . .
yes, wisdom only you can give.

Be it, too, your vivid vision,
with your sacred flame aglow . . .
walking on, hands high,
and freedom
breathing in your soul,
assured
the breath of god awaits . . .
your Sagessence story.

Tending the Fire

🔥

Chapter 1

The Sage Coming of Age

Birth of the Sage

Unlike mother's third babe,
I am now taller with breadth.
I speak my own language,
articulate and confident.
Tracings of age etch my face.
Both palms are now carved
with deep lines of a lifetime.
My heart, under fuller breasts,
nurtures dreams for the world.

Belly now supple, round—
with fullness suggesting yet
another kind of birthing,
I look into the reflection
of my mirrored naked body
uncertain of what is beyond
this incarnate illumination.
It is as if I have conceived
a life I am yet meant to live.

Inside I hear whispers
from a soft, husky voice—
Your time has come.
Let go, surrender to the
powerful pulsing rhythm

urging birth of your sage.
Reconcile the blueprint
of your life, and beget the path
of your woman soul.

Now with womanly fullness,
I sense the inner push of
a profound metamorphosis.
I summon my keen intuition,
open my well-traveled heart,
and claim seasoned wisdom
of a matured woman cloaked
in years of refined texture and
intricate tapestry of a sacred life.

Once again,
I am filled
with another
first precious breath,
and now
I know
my long-awaited sage
has been given
her birth.

Body Temple

Reflecting on my mother's 91 years,
I bow reverently to the essence
of the woman of my beginning—
who willingly nurtured Divine seeds
to create my way.
I prayerfully breathe in gratitude
for the gift of her body temple
that offered my life.

Beholding her sacred fullness—with child,
she knew when her all had been given.
When the miracle that was meant to be
could no longer be withheld,
she birthed my life with might and courage,
releasing in cries of completion,
letting go from the well
of her warm water and nurturing blood.

Now, after decades of living,
I prayerfully breathe in gratitude
for the gift of my body temple
that continues to offer me life.
As a seasoned woman
impregnated by years of living,

I behold my own sacred fullness—with sage,
anticipating birth of another great purpose.

From creations cast by the sacred thread
that flows from the One Great Fertile Womb,
from generations of the past
into the greater good of the future . . .
comes urgency to birth Wisdom's legacy
for the eager evolution of this soul
that whispers its desires
in the heart of my body temple.

Breath of Knowing

There are times a woman
will say, *no*, to those she loves,
carry no judgment of her own,
and in her next breath
affirm, *yes*,
to the bold voice
of the wise sage within.

As for me . . .
I will follow my dreams,
kindly dismiss what no longer
I choose to carry,
let my heart speak its truth,
and give to life the only gift
I have to give—my truest self.

My eyes will be on the owl
as dear ones call out to me,
Please come back . . .
stay the same,
understanding they do not want
their beliefs challenged,
hoping their world will not change.

It's no wonder they pull at my heart,
yank on my mind,
with arms around my ankles,
clinging tight for a perfect woman
standing for generations past,
perplexed
by wisdom of my intuitive choices.

As for me . . .
I quietly breathe, *no*,
knowing I will not go on as before.
I feel it in my bones.
My breath speaks new truth,
and the sage in me again says, *yes*,
to this primal breath of knowing.

Come to Your Life

Regardless of what you think
your life should have been,
or what you have believed
could have been better choices,
or what voices said to tempt
your heart to turn and run;
regardless of what you know,
what you don't know,
or what you wish to understand—

Come to your life today
with an open, healed heart,
allow your dear soul
to reflect its deeper truth,
increase your capacity to love,
emulate your unique wisdom.
Simply come . . .
with greater appreciation
for all that has been before.

Come to your life filled,
not empty.
Wrap your arms around you.
Kneel to the mysterious calls

you hear from the gods.
Arrive at your place shouting
to the Universe to prepare
for your living an even more
exquisite version of you.

Essence

Who is this spirit
that resides in me?
What is this essence,
this inexhaustible fire
that burns throughout
my vast eternities?

What is this warmth,
this light that burned
before my father's sperm
and mother's ovum,
before my first breath,
first sight and sound?

Does this It really
remain pure, powerful
and untouched
by people, places, things
and tough miracles
of this world I came to?

Is It truly safe from
my greatest doubts
and disappointments,

fears and resentments,
and even loves that
sculpt my path in life?

Does it say It is—
my power of presence,
my power of god within,
my timeless, omnipresent
effervescence that
will not, does not, cannot—

And is not altered by
what I say, what I do,
who or what I know,
where I am, who I love?
Is it an eternal flame
sourcing essence of my life?

Hand Open

Our time of birth
is the beginning
of truly another
stunning crisis
because all growing,
all developing,
in mother's womb
is then complete.

For us, a tiny one,
we must go on
if we are to live,
if we are to thrive,
if we are to grow,
to develop on Earth,
we have no choice
but to leave.

Mystery's hand open,
we must trust
what is not
known to be true.
We must get out,
move on into light

of a new day,
of a new epoch.

This is the truth
of who we are.
This is the law
of our universe.
Predictable,
we know this—
it is written in the
script of our soul.

Maybe, we begin
to remember
our births and deaths
call us, hand open.
Then, without a cry,
we come to trust
what seems uncertain
to be true.

Phoenix

Rise up,
rise up like a phoenix
from your own fire,
a fire you agreed to,
the gods arced,
you stepped into.

It's a fire
calling on forgiveness,
deep transformative love,
a burning away
of all that
is not for good.

Rise up,
take the new vision,
turn away from all
that does not give life
to the liberated one
you forever are.

Calm waters
wait to take you,
swallow you completely,

'til you look up into it,
rays of light luring you
to gasp new breath.

Seeking the Sage

You seek beyond yourself
with a searching heart,
yet with a sleepy mind.
And, the wise sage asks,
For whom are you seeking?

You wander the fields
searching furrows and hills;
outward you go, ignorant
to the illusion of your desires,
Awaken from your sleep.

Befriend the quiet inside,
let your eyes grow large,
see the illuminating glow,
turn an ear to the soft voice,
Return to your own gate.

Nothing can compare to
the genius deep within—
wisdom gained from decades,
messages waiting to be heard,
It is the seeker who is sought.

Come to fully understand
that the one sought lives in
your own sacred homeland,
the one you are looking for,
The sage sought is you.

Standing in the Fire

Standing in the fire,
I pray it not go out.
My heart says,
Let it burn.
Let it engulf my thoughts,
my ideas,
and dreams,
each inspiration
that the muse has sparked.
Transform each into
unique beauty and art
of new stories
that desire to finally be born
out of the fires of creativity.

It says,
Stand in my fire.
Have faith in the flames,
blow breath on the embers,
don't let the author of your life
perish in cold cinders
because you were afraid,
or did not listen
with an open heart.

Trust the absolute genius
of that which longs
to be conceived by you,
that longs to be born
out of the fires of heaven.

Pray
Let it burn!

The Sage Comes

After years and years,
finally . . .
the wise sage comes.

With compassionate acceptance
your sage welcomes everything back—
all you wished would be different,
old wounds, scars, and limps,
lost innocence, possessions, loves,
wildness you and others tried to tame,
dreams that remained formless,
fears that attempted conquest,
humiliation that nearly crippled,
grief leaving remnants of quiet anger,
confusion that disturbed your path,
relationships that eroded with time.

Time is what the inner sage says
is needed to finally understand
that all mattered, all was necessary,
for a deep, artful texture and
rich, transfixing, colorful grain
of your true divine magnificence
to emerge from the one and only

truly jaded shadow—
that is the horrific misperception
that you should have been perfect,
or whatever should be different.
No, not even so.

After years and years,
finally . . .
you will hear your sage speak.

Everything brought you to now.
Now, hold each morsel of your life
with tenderness,
honor as gems—
otherwise, wisdom is shamed,
unique creations are dishonored,
authenticity risks being aborted.
And, with tender self-compassion,
open to the great embrace
that allows immersion
into true love—you loving you,
that the gods gifted as only yours.

Continue

The sage says, this we do lest
we succumb to the madness
of severing ourselves from peace.
Thus, we must thank the wounds,
the scars, and the limps.
Choose forgiveness and love,
set free wildness that seeks
to ride dreams into new realities,
live passionately, confidently,
bid farewell to all that trusts not
the absolute beauty of our lives.
Then, graciously bow to wisdom—

That bequeaths the sage's call.

Truth

I look in the mirror
and I see
the absolute truth.

And, I wonder,
Are the lines
etched in my face
showing
a stunning legacy,
and silvery, graying temples
not really
supposed to participate
in the ever-evolving
truth of life?

Who or what was it
that settled
truth should be different?

Winter's Light

This Winter's day,
I know not
my unfolding path in Spring,
yet I trust a sense of hibernating
with the Mother of Spring's creation.

Like tall Douglas firs,
I wait . . .
believing that Spring waits,
wanting to breathe fertile air again . . .
reaching to the heavens
in mysterious, amazing ways,
up from wet, generative land
where we both dream
to burst forth new branches.

I believe,
like in the floors of the forest,
muted earthy hues
in the floors of my living
will once again transform
into the vibrant richness
that only happens by sun's light
rising from Winter's day
cast on Spring's awakening.

Dare I choose to trust
the wisdom of Winter's light
gently urging
awaking from hibernation?
Dare I open my heart
to its rhythmic invitation—
to be changed by a luminosity
that gently seeks birth
in my life?

Tending the Fire

Chapter 2

Flames of Authenticity

A Day to Let Go

Today is a day
to let go
of all that has been.
In extraordinary moments,
with this one as witness,
leaves simply let go
of all their life has
been in seasons past.

From voluptuous buds
alive with vibrancy
of succulent green,
sensuous yellow
to hot fiery orange
then majestic red,
they now relinquish
to a graceful descent:

Turning away,
floating, twirling,
flirtatiously dancing,
gliding up,
drifting down,
veined edges to the heavens,

gracefully suspended,
without breath at all.

In these mysterious
final moments—
is this what living
has prepared us for:
a grand surrender of
letting to into the
soft, cool lap of Gaia,
our holy, sacred retreat?

Today is a day
I dare ask my question,
*What else do I
desire of me?*
Listening intently,
a soft echo rises
in the cool, damp,
mountain breeze.

It is the simple sigh
of the awed witness—
yes, also suspended

Continue

like without breath.
I wait in the leaves
for an answer, breathing,
What else do I
desire of me?

Alchemist

I have come to realize
one of the greatest journeys
is one of moving past fear,
accepting with new eyes,
discovering a grander view
that desires expression
in and through my life.

Even when my feet tremble,
heart throbbing in my ears,
I can still hear
that inner voice
urging me
to trust vistas unknown . . .
if I will just surrender.

Whether it be in quietness
or in chaos of uncertainty,
I will again feel
the one thing
that will not
leave me alone . . .
a fire in my belly—

Continue

An alchemist leading me on,
melding me into the masterpiece
of an even higher calling . . .
if I will just surrender
to the gods
and drink in trust
like fresh, cool water.

Autumn Is Gone

I raise the window shade
and clearly see,
autumn is gone, and
winter has come.

After a dense, dark night,
I gaze across the Hood Canal,
rumpled pajamas hanging
on my still tired body.
My weathered toes curl
into the fiber of the carpet
nailed to the cool, wood floor
as I squint at Canadian geese
in perfect, sweeping formation
across a majestic silhouette.

I sigh, captured by the beauty
of the Olympic mountains
now snowcapped this morning.
I wince for the weary grass
cloaked in crisp white crystals
for the first time this season.
Heavy grayness hovers over
the water in the ebbing canal,

Continue

yet it is artistically rimmed
in a soothing hazy pink.

Running my fingers through
my eschewed hair, I wonder,
Can I still love my life?
Can I find treasures in winter,
knowing with raw respect that
She has now claimed Her season?
Standing silently in my bedroom,
I welcome Her husky voice,
and pray my soul be content
during my own late season.

I hold my arms around me
as I feel it in my bones . . .
indeed, my autumn is gone
and winter grace has come.

Fallow Time

Winter darkness comes home
deep within the stilled soul
in the quiet, cold, long nights
while the forest floor lies dormant
under the dead growth of summer.

Recall last spring's greening and
lively vibrancy that followed, and
all that withered from fall's harvest.
Now shelter your dear heart,
rest in the furry crescent of
your own warm hospitality,
breathe in arcs of light promising
to defy such eager deep darkness.

Bow to dreams, worries and wars,
disappointments, accomplishments,
and ways of being that served you—
all guides to Love's transformation.
Lay them all on glowing cinders
of earlier seasons, and silently
bless the ash that carries the
stories and teachings to heaven.

Continue

Open wide your cloak and offer
beauty of nakedness to shadows
cast by evening's flickering fire.
Stand on the hearth of pure potentiality—
empty as a flute without a melody,
clear as a mirror reflecting no thing,
bare as a page before a thought
is scribed into the written word.

Remember, the magic of Winter
is potency to impregnate new life—
seeds sourced by god's breath in
rich fallow soil of your rare essence.
Can you celebrate the dense darkness,
bless the light that will prevail, and
welcome god's gift of gestation that
nurtures its mysterious sacredness?

Winter darkness will come home
deep within your stilled soul
in the quiet, cold, long nights, and
your soul will surely soon quicken
with heartbeats of god's new life.

Fire from Heaven

Bathing in this fire
I let go of everything…
except my willingness—

Willingness, that is,
to be transformed by fire,
confident divine mystery
resides in my soul.
My fire is perfect
and it's flames infinite,
wise and creative.
It reveals truth of who I am,
boundless perfection,
complete
and whole.

No thing that I have done,
said,
or thought, can rise up
against these flames.
No thing has power over,
nor confines me now.
There is no memory of fear,
no judgment,

Continue

nor condemnation,
that can survive
this sea of fire.

It fuels my intense desire
to be free.
I surrender to its pure light
striking into all
I perceived as error.
Nothing is held against me.
Every limiting thought, belief
and attitude,
every perceived foible is
transformed by
this fire from heaven.

Forgotten Contentment

One sleepy eye opened.
I sighed,
peering through morning dew,
wet and beading
on a bedroom window
that frames the guardian fir tree—
the towering one,
that has been a natural companion
through years of living
on this coastal hillside.

Slowly, my other eye followed.
I squinted into the early coral dawn
bathing the Olympic Mountains.
My fingers grazed across
the warm nap of soft fleece sheets
as I became keenly aware
of an inner silence . . .
a sweet comfort,
like the quiet aftermath of
a stilled Midwest plains storm.

Perplexed, I sighed
into a stare of curiosity.

Continue

Is this my soul's quiet breathing
after years of wrangling
with that which it agreed to
before my mother's conception—
this breathing in,
breathing out,
without the ageless gnawing grip
of some thing?

Is this the pure essence
of the soul's autumn honey
that now permeates the combs
of this body, this mind,
clearing for its sweet spirit
to finally, . . . to finally
come back home to the queen's hive
of forgotten contentment?
Is this the place of love's divine warmth
before I was begotten?

And I ask the wise guardian tree,
Is it now that I live or,
is it now that I can die?

Home

Come
to that
which longs
for you
to be fully home
to all
that you are.

Your home
awaits
with open doors,
the threshold flush;
you
need not
stumble in.

House of Faith

Tell me how
to be at home
with faith.

I know what love is like—
that exhilarating freedom to
soar in tandem with another,
careening through
every room of the heart.

And joy—
the rise of enlivening
contagious amusement,
felicity, and bliss that
fills the rafters of the soul.

Even hope—
eternal longing that lives
in mind's hearth, fanning flames
that whatever will somehow,
someday be different.

Of course, gratitude—
singing in various verses

of abundant well-being,
is always ready to echo
through chambers of my heart.

But faith—
how do I know It
for which god awakens me
in my bed and whispers,
It is all about faith.

When will faith pass over
my soil and notice the
river rocks in my path?
What will it take to come
to my weathered door?

So faith, . . . I say,
Just bolt right on in
and don't you even dare
hide in old dusty closets
or dim corners in the hall.

Come to my dining table.
Heap your overflowing

Continue

cornucopia in bowls and plates.
Sit and eat with me,
you and I, dear faith.

I will welcome you
like a long lost friend—
this time we will not sleep
but become dazed and drunk
on aged wine of bold trust.

Then after morning comes,
you will reside with me
and I will reside with you—
yes, we will co-abide
together in my house of faith.

And gratefully,
you will be at home with me,
dear faith.

Infinite Creation

There is no time
when I am finished,
nor when the gods
are finished with me.

If eternal life's story
means anything at all,
it means that I am
an infinite creation.

Is not creation alive
through all stages,
through all ages,
of this lavish life?

Like a lush rose,
letting go in autumn,
it's bare nakedness
plans summer splendor.

Am I not also a work
of such divine art,
sharing in one endless
perpetual embryo?

Continue

If heavens are infinite,
I too must be
a boundless dream
of plotting holy ones.

Then, it surely
must be known,
in each ending is
again my beginning.

Old Dreams

What *were* your hopes and dreams
before standing on this side of
between what might be possible
and what has happened by now?

From hoping for money to pay bills,
saving children from alluring magic,
to grasping long, hard hours may have
meant more to you than to others?

What exquisite pieces and parts
were lost in hungry shadows, and
hidden in matters that truly risked
extinction of your one original life?

Time is a trickster—an illusion of plenty
So, now is an age for edgy questions:
*What would your future-self recognize
as happiness ... as joy once fantasized?*

What abandoned desires linger like
stubble seeds in fields of your heart?
Can you trust old dreams ache for you—
wait for you to confess they still live?

This Box

Here, in this box of my unlived life,
I look back, imagining what from here.
A desire for stillness engulfs me while
I immerse in hot, steaming spring water,
freezing cold pinching my cheeks red,
wind howling through the swaying firs.

Nature patiently offers this, then that—
its stories, its parables over and again,
like snowflakes falling to metamorphosis,
and flora's respite offering winter solace,
this pause in my life, this strange place,
where wonder is all I have to my name.

Many parts of life over, future not seen,
a box of not anymore and not quite yet.
I rise up through the mysterious steam,
my divine breath clouded pure white.
I cautiously emerge from burbling heat
feeling ice form under my wet, bare feet.

I hesitantly lift one foot, then the other
fearing I will freeze in place like stone,
embarking a snowy path, naked-hearted,

toward thriving in an ensuing creation,
embryonic, pushing out through walls,
casting away this box of my unlived life.

Who is this Child

Who is this child
the wise ones speak of?
Whom will it be
who will greet her,
if not me?

Who will cherish her,
know her wonder, her joy,
keep her near, and
let her come real,
if not me?

They say it is her curiosity
that inspires,
that will give me fresh life
to see, hear, speak and do
another surprising thing.

It is she who will lead me
to newness of life,
since that is who she is
they say,
a pure, pristine being.

Can I believe it is
the child of my beginning
who holds the power
to take me through
my next great birth?

Aye, can I imagine,
as they promise,
it is she
who will lead me through
my last great death?

Who is this child
the wise ones speak of?
Whom will it be
who will take Her,
if not me?

Tending the Fire

🔥

Chapter 3

Flames of Passion

Faces of Eternity

Through a fog of rapid living
during so many decades
comes a welcomed quiet, . . .
yet, old disquieted memories
find a way to enter my heart.

Who are these dear images
emerging from long ago,
with innocent, intense eyes
that once seeded dreams in
a younger woman I once was?

Who are they after all this time?
Are they imps with simple curiosity
arising from tiny, treasured places
as I recall choices I did not make,
choices I did, paths taken and not?

These inquiring voices will not
be silenced—as if I even would.
I ask, *Are we imbued in eternity,*
having come together before,
and perhaps yet to circle again?

Maybe it's an enduring desire
of five billion years, or so—
timeless sojourners deepening
in the Omnipresent Mystery . . .
having once known pure joy,

Returning, reaching out once again,
like hesitant fingers touching
dots of delicate autumn dew
on the eternal face of a beloved,
simply not wanting to go away.

Grand Love

She was 92.
Her beloved was 88.
They warmed me
like few lovers have.
Their tenderness,
respect
and gratitude
prevailed throughout
their late season days.
And only like
old sweethearts can,
they always discovered
satisfying ways
to express steadfast,
tender love;
to share gems
of intimacy
that come with time,
and grace hearts
with fulfillment.

Growing older
day by day,
they beheld each other

with grand love,
a mystery
nothing could deter.
Although years claimed
their harsh mark
in many unfriendly,
unkind ways,
gazing into each other's
wise eyes,
holding each other's
feeble hands,
truly dismissed
any naive notion
that seasoned love
could possibly belong
to man and woman
of their youth.

The world yearns
for what they shared,
like writing
I love you
on plaid, flannel backs
in the night,

Continue

stroking white hair
with gnarled fingers,
blowing kisses,
through windowpanes,
eyes twinkling
with mischievous,
ancient laughter.
Their endearment
was not for taking
but to be witnessed
as they continued
their art of forgiveness,
their joy of being
dearly loved.

They knew their breath
was precious life,
and did not allow
a loving moment
to escape
their few fragile days.
They engaged
soulful pleasures,
ever imbued

by simple delights.
And, like old lovers
with new eyes,
they gazed tenderly
under drooping lids
into windows
of each other's
dear soul,
treasuring grand love—
their legacy
of love's sweet mystery.

Love of Life

I used to think
it was one person
with me
that would bring love,
would bring contentment,
joy of belonging,
gratification
that I was seeking.

My desires have changed;
past days are more
than yet to come,
my seasoned life ripened
like soft delicate sauciness
of sweet, matured
blackberries
in late September.

Now that I am this old,
I desire love of life;
not just any love, but
moments I lose myself
completely, for days…
not in just moments of

fleeting
short-lived orgasm.

My heart swells
with implausible joy
when my fingers slowly
draw over a body I love,
trace edges of a rose,
outline ridges of sand
artistically arranged
on sea's shore.

I intend to kiss my days,
moment by moment,
with new eyes, new ears,
celebrating my life's
incredulous beauty,
becoming drunk on joy,
gobbled up
by love of life.

Love's Tough Miracle

Whether we quarrel with love,
wrangle with human limitations
or perhaps misunderstand god,
there are times each of us
must travel a solitary path
until we are humbled
by love's tough miracle
teaching us what aspects
of ourselves are separated from
the true nature of who we are.

I have heard that fiery courage
unleashed by the soul's sage
just may spark burning down walls
of an invincible armored heart,
gaining entry to all those pieces
that long for union once again.
I hear that after she has her way,
it is the Queen Sage who kisses
the back of our hands,
and quietly, patiently, waits.

Could it be . . .
in such moments of time

it was my soul's sage that
unleashed love's tough miracle,
set me on fire,
dismantled my invincible heart
and taught me
to lovingly gather
the cinders of my life into
the blessed journey of *I am?*

My heart ponders the query,
as I notice a moist lip imprint
on the back of my hands,
like dew on autumn roses.
Is it the sage's invitation,
a wise cairn,
inviting another way,
changing my life forever,
blessing me
by love's tough miracle?

My Anchor

I am captured by the sea's spirit,
taken by her immensity,
enticed by mysteries of worlds
hidden below rising and falling
of her elegant cadence,
of wild stirrings,
of creations only imagined.

I come to her shores for strength,
to cast my cares,
to touch drops of understanding,
to believe I am one with greatness.
I feel the soothing heartbeat
of her rhythmic waves
slowly calm my racing mind.

Squinting my eyes in awe,
I walk meditatively beside her
clearing my thoughts,
buoying my spirits
as she fills the well of my soul,
as I sigh into sweet release,
as I breathe in salty inspiration.

She opens a portal of wisdom
releasing a blessing of insights,
drawing me away from
misguided ways
of my darting mind,
of an unsettled heart,
of cast-away dreams.

I go to her seeking a feeling
of connection with god,
listening for even one word—
a message that I need
to let go of regrets,
to believe in the unknown,
to live life passionately.

I love her.
And, in her presence
I anchor my life.

October Dance

Light passes through
wistful October leaves,
casts through the window,
fondles the old wood floor
gently bringing me
to my clumsy feet.
Graceful shadows,
like a debonair lover
palms turned upward,
invite me to dance
before it's too late,
before my memory
doesn't still remember.

I rise from my chair
reaching out into it,
accepting the invitation,
slowly beginning to twirl,
feeling this bit of joy
as a blue gauzy dress
floats to and fro
gently sweeping me.
And, I see in my mind
sequins in the sunlight

catching glimpses of
old tender moments
before I don't remember.

One Thing

One thing I must say,
You are my Beloved—
and I know not why
the gods smiled on me
generously gifting
this everlasting fire
in my belly of being.

One thing I will tell,
You are my heart's manna—
inimitably nourishing love
which cannot flourish in
the absence of our souls
converging in this journey
through immortal time.

One thing I whisper,
You are my deep passion—
so come, I welcome you
to my innermost hearth
which is fomented by
the Divine wind of
our life-giving breath.

One thing I give you,
I give you me—
I stand before you
without pretense,
my tender story naked,
humbly knowing this
is all I have to give.

Sacred Thirst

Oh, sacred thirst—
the familiar, unfulfilled longing
that entraps the heart.
Once satisfied,
it relishes cherished content
and revels
in magnificent fulfillment
of what is hoped to be eternal.

And then slowly,
the quenched desire dissipates
into quiet gnawing once again
at the corners of lips,
in the recesses of the heart,
as the satisfying glory melts
into the embrace of thirst
for one more delicious goblet
poured full at the table
of the dear beloved.

Then again,
the brave heart relinquishes itself
to an ever-magnificent contentment,
though it will most certainly

fall in love again with longing—
like sweetness that desires
to infuse late harvested grapes
for sacred wine of the goddesses.

Salt

I stepped onto the sand
at nearly sunset,
sighing into a gentle breeze
that carried the gift of salt—
caressing my face,
invigorating my lungs,
enlivening my senses,
preserving evening with
absolute cathartic magic.

Gazing across the sea,
piquant salt of lovers
rushed into my memory,
shaking my heart
with tender, zesty emotions
of a time when life
was pregnant with life
and nothing mattered
but the sweat of loving.

In remembering . . .
warm crystalline tears
fell slowly, gently
over my cool cheeks

making broad turns
over the bow of my lip,
seeping salt onto my tongue,
as I stood silently in awe
of its mysterious nature.

What if salt's teaching
is to consciously savor
it's gifts that beckon
abundant love of life—
embracing earthiness,
seasoning new horizons,
inspiring gusto for
a spicy, flavorful life until
our last and final taste?

Did I hear the sea whisper,
Yes!, with its invisible breath?
Is this the teaching for
the sage's salt-infused life—
love life,
embrace earthiness,
season new horizons,

Continue

inspire gusto
for a spicy, flavorful life—

Until my . . .
or your . . .
last and final taste?

Story of Intimacy

I yearn
to live a story of intimacy,
beyond my youth,
beyond mid-life,
beyond society's meaning.
I desire to be deeply known,
yet fear being known
both at the same time.
It is my profound need,
like food to eat,
water to drink,
air to breathe.

I reach for waiting arms
of deep intimacy.
At times I touch its sweetness
while thinking,
I may keep secrets my own.
Yet, the voice of intimacy
asks me to share
tender stories of my heart,
of my mind,
of my soul,
share them with another
imperfect human being—

Continue

Allow another to discover
what moves me, inspires me,
drives me, hurts me,
makes me smile and sigh,
what I am running toward
and running from,
what I whisper to the gods at night,
and what silent, impish enemies
still reside deep within,
what wildness I harbor,
and what wonderful dreams
still wait deep in my heart.

What is your story?
Do you have a deep need
to be known—
to be discovered,
and re-discovered
over and over in a lifetime?
If you do, take my hand
and don't go away—

I promise to not turn from you

and perhaps, dear one,

together we will discover

a new story of intimacy.

This I Know

This I know for certain—
love is tough.
Love's potency is nearly indestructible.
It is patient and sustains
with hopeful openheartedness.

I know love does not give up easily.
Yet, when it does
it surrenders exhausted,
emptying exhalation
without in-breath.

Knowing intolerable aridity,
love may give way,
settle face down
into long, thin grooves
in one's heart—

And there, . . . dissipate,
day by day,
into dry,
impermeable
lifelessness.

I know love appears to surrender
to completion.
Yet, when it does,
something other than love
has seeped into cracks of the heart—

Distorting its essence,
warping its beauty.
And, love knows
that
does not belong to itself.

Then god paces softly.
She moistens love's soul
with Her tears,
and becomes
a lover with fallow time.

This I know.

This Old Man

He came to me…
a white-haired, dark eyed,
strikingly intelligent man,
said he was crazy about me,
even at my old age.
Yet, I feared him,
wondered if I dare trust him,
not to mention it has been
forty-two years since I laid
my then flawless, eager body
next to the heat of a man.

This old man says
he needs to be with me;
I will sing you to sleep
every night until I die,
I will wake you in morning
with my breath in your hair.
I gasp at his dreams,
tempted, and yet I fear us.
Then I drop my clothes,
bear my battle ground body
and say, *What shall we sing?*

Tending the Fire

Chapter 4

Flames of Compassion

Day Break

Early light dares pierce tight
closed openings of my tired eyes.
I hear ground squirrels chatter,
racing back and forth across
boards foliaged in pink clematis,
while robins celebrate morning—
bopping up . . . down . . . as they do
in exuberant, tenacious staccato.

Is it truly a new dawning, though
I fear yet dreaming in night?
Could it be that cool, sweet salt
of evening's air prayerfully swept
over the warmth of my dark cover
empathically christening this day?
Could it be in one dogged moment
daybreak's light bid sorrow farewell?

And, could it be this day break
compassionately
entreats sweet living again?

Endings

Children don't worry about death.
As one,
I never imagined my own.
My grandma died when she was old,
yet
quite younger than I am now.

At my age, there is kind freedom
in believing, trustily,
that I have died over and again.
And,
like wise children,
there is no need to worry, because…

What do I *really* know is an ending?
And, what is truly a beginning?
Since, in me,
my grandmother has breathed again,
over and over,
in so many mysterious ways.

Ghost of Love

The moment I first saw you
I knew you knew me.
You knocked on the door
of my soul and I let you in.
You were like a part of me
reaching back to a place
I had forgotten,
reaching back to a place
I hadn't remembered,
a place where I had learned
the truth about coming alive,
yet left behind in earlier time.

It was your gaze into my soul,
your embrace and love,
your unfailing belief in me
that was luscious balm
for my tender heart.
It was there
I discovered faith,
like a young child at sea
finally discovering a safe harbor—
that sweet resting place
where storms would not deter
the sweet purity of life.

That bit of Universe time—
a time for us,
graced dear love,
then pierced with deep grief as
I watched your ship leave my harbor,
gliding away on the seas
one winter morning.
I watched as the beauty of you
grew smaller in the distance,
as the swells of life rose and fell
until the fading horizon
welcomed you into her arms.

The harbor that was ours
was where I learned about truth,
where I learned that
the winds of love could
steady my mast,
a wind I trusted to anchor my life.
Yet, the winds of change
and rumbling bore tides
can also tear a mast to shreds,
unknot tight sturdy ties,
its trade can set opposing sails,
and hurl about a precious life.

Continue

So, as it comes to pass,
I occasionally open the hull
in my mind to see
if you are still there,
and what I see
is a ghost of love—
one that smiles tenderly,
one that reaches to touch
edges of my damp cheeks.
And, when I reach for you,
I only feel a touch of cool sea air
press ever so gently into me.

Then, hesitantly, I turn away
still grateful
still thankful
for learning how to love well;
still grateful
still thankful
for the teacher who gave me life.

Great Masters

As surely as . . .

Brown eight-eyed orb weavers
float another silk line
to the October winds,

And

Little purple and white crocus
hardily push through winter's snow
as promise of new life,

Great blue heron will arrive
at woodland nesting grounds
spring after spring—

And

I will pause a summertime eve
recalling bittersweet
and tender farewells in winter.

As surely as . . .

Continue

Great masters keenly practice
nature's seasons calling for another
web, blossom, and twig—

I will offer gratitude for each
tender memory that desires
renewal in my heart,

Season after season.

Grieve

Grieve
until the candle goes out,
until its sides lay open,
gaping,
from the heat of fire
on walls of wax.

Grieve
for all you thought lost,
for all you hoped for,
stunned,
charred by the wick
of true forgiveness.

Grieve
until it is all over,
until heart stops heaving,
quiets,
rests in the smell
of gray, black smoke.

Grieve
until all the stories
are safely sheltered,

Continue

forever,
on pages, in chapters
of a beloved life.

Heart of Grief

When heart falls into the grip of grief,
it cannot dismiss hopes from the past
which continue to tantalize elusively
like seductive smoke escaping in thin air.
Grief wrestles with tomorrow's fantasy—
dreams that become simply vapor
and cannot be visualized as real…like
illusive clouds, dissipating, untouchable.

Standing raw with taunting memories,
high stakes paid by an exhausted heart,
grief washes over the contour of now,
drenching the soul in present moment.
Heart aches while fighting for stability.
Certainty of anything becomes fable,
except the jagged pain that persists
begging patience with impending change.

Can a courageous heart let go of illusion,
grapple with grief's agonizing company,
invite its mulish healer to be kind,
and surrender to honest, mysterious reality?
This is the query . . .

Continue

that yanks at the tender heart of grief.
Thus is the query . . .
that begs healing of a heart and soul.

Heartland of Our Souls

I will stay with you in this place
no matter what you need
or how long it takes
for gain of strength
to move on again.
I will remain as your companion,
whiling time away,
seeking calm solace,
feeding on leftovers in stubbles,
bedding in tall reeds of cool rivers.

There is no need to go anywhere
nor return
to my place called home.
I will wait on one leg,
then another,
in the hospitality of quiet blinds,
patiently keeping loving watch
with uninterrupted gaze,
attending compassionately,
guarding your peace of heart.

Of course, that is until . . .
in an instinctual moment,

Continue

like crimson-crowned cranes,
majestic wings spanned wide,
bodies stretched long and lean,
we fly toward fields flourishing
with abundant harvests,
beyond the beyond,
heavens welcoming our soar
into another intuitive unknown.

Yes, you can count on me.
I will stay with you until,
like crimson-crowned cranes
called to dances
in other fertile fields,
either you . . .
or I . . .
take flight from this place
to another land—
the heartland of our souls.

Letting Go

As evening came in his latter years,
his heart wrangled with letting go—
letting go of possessions,
ideals of health, infinite independence,
and life itself.

Letting go of dreams
incomplete, unfinished,
that escaped from his fragile reality—
replacing desires with mustered hope
of just one more day doing what he loved.

He burrowed in the comfort, the safety,
of his rocking chair in a quiet living room,
wisely surrendering
to honest gratefulness,
to fulfillment in reminiscing joy.

With soft smiles on his thin lips,
he gazed tenderly into faces of those he loved
while struggling to let go,
still wanting to hold on,
yet surrendering to the evening of his life.

Resolve

Turning a tough memory
over and again in my mind
is like turning a stone
over again in my hand
looking for an opening to
find resolve stuck inside.

The war in my head
can't be counted on, nor
memory counted on either.
Time is a fallacious friend.
Everything dissolves and
everything soon will die.

All around looks like spring.
Robins gather, pecking away;
showers come boding life,
but it only looks like spring.
For me, it's truly late
maybe fall, perhaps winter.

How do I find resolve
before the curtain closes?
My prayer is not to stay stuck,

gawking for some opening,
turning a tough memory
over and again in my mind.

Sacred Friend

When I stand in the
middle of the fire,
will you come near and
stand by my side?
Will you dare hold
my hand in yours?

When I wrangle
with the fire's wisdom,
and perhaps question god,
will you look directly into
reflections in my eyes
and see Her perfection?

When I am humbled by
miracles of heat teaching
that as ice becomes water,
fire also changes form,
will you trust the truth
of who I am becoming?

When I am consumed
by hungry, wild flames,
will you remain with me,

wipe sweat from my brow,
and eagerly applaud my
expanding transformation?

Will you be a sacred friend,
encourage me to live me,
celebrate my new incarnation—
knowing my Divine spark
certainly can no more die . . .
than god can.

Sovereignty

She says her old husband
has found renewed passion;
he discovered a new love,
a delightful drive and reason
in his every day of silence.
Puzzles have saved his life—
and, no doubt, hers as well.

Yes, every morning now...
at ninety-nine years of age,
he shuffles to his workshop.
Hours tick by as he finds
a piece that makes sense,
fits the space, falls in place,
creates an artful pattern.

Barely lifting his face,
he graciously thanks her
for morning creamed coffee,
or placing a sparse lunch
by his gnarled brainy hands
as his eyes search, seeking
before it's too late to finish.

She is thankful for his find,
granting her relished hours
again, after so very long.
Her private desire quenched,
she guiltlessly lets him be,
cherishing forgotten freedom,
life-giving time for herself.

Finally, after six years raging
like a migratory bird, caged …
after the kids took her car away
on the night of her 90th birthday,
after smoke curled from candles,
after hideous laugher hunkered
up in the living room ceiling—

She says, now she too has won
renewed passion, joy as well,
salvaged sweet liberty—
moments for choice, free will
to simply walk her garden path.
She says puzzles saved her life,
granted sovereignty again.

Two Words

Unlike birds of the air,
fish of the sea,
trees bent by harsh
unforgiving winds,
I've struggled for wisdom
to accept courage,
the backbone to say
two words... I'm sorry.

Words may mean little
yet take me off a hook,
they can be complex
leaving many traces —
like yellow slivers
from dandelion heads
between two fingers
staining my hard pinch.

Wordless, heart aches;
so, I bow to you and
simply say, *I'm sorry*.
Hands on my heart,
I can see the grass
slowly lift up from

barren timeworn circles
my feet have trampled.

Grace quiets doubts —
if I were wrong
or if I were right.
Then, like the birds
the fish and the trees,
I feel freedom again
because of the rarity
of two words, *I'm sorry.*

Tending the Fire

Chapter 5

Flames of Vision

A River Through My Life

Remember, my child

You are a river through my life.
I feel you coming through me.
I marvel at your significance,
your powerful, inspiring presence.
I am awed as the gods welcome
the coursing of the natural flow
of your fresh life across the land.
I want to hold you forever and
yet, there is no sense to even try—
perhaps, your imprint is my gift.

At times,

I have imagined holding on
to loved ones, places, things—
even chapters of my life that
enlivened the sleeping giant
in the deep bed of my soul.
I know sweet gifts of living,
like sharing this life with you,
will never leave heart's banks.
Therefore, I will tenderly hold
dear treasures each gift defines.

Meanwhile,

As I gaze into sparkling pools
of your curious, cosmic eyes,
maybe the treasure I see in you
is that which I can give myself—
trust no matter my seasoned age,
I lay my life open like a river
whose nature deems no shelter,
nor ways to withhold its path,
or to keep ripples of light from
reflecting radiance in the world.

Therefore, remember my child,

The gods do not deem ways to
withhold your divine creations,
now dare I ask, *Not even mine?*
Thus, might our lives emulate
grand rivers, flowing freely,
converging watermarks with ease.
Might we create unique, rare
tributaries in this world because
our souls joined in the journey,
flowing to the ocean of eternity.

Brooding

Winter,
rising from mature darkness,
offers its faithful bidding
for brooding reflection…
a time to pause
for deep stories to find my lips,
a time to gather
around a hearth of friendship,
a time to surrender,
fully exposed,
to the north light of winter.

Curiously,
I find myself longing
for this blackness of Solstice,
for the peace it brings.
I am raw with musing,
searching deep understandings;
my life's autumn is complete,
like a last chapter's page
damp with ink,
drying…
ready to turn for the next.

What shards of light
are found in darkness?
What stunning stories
will a final season bring?
I sigh into deep pause,
I quiet…
my soul waits to be heard,
as I draw in replenishment
with brooding renewal,
taking in this clean, pristine
breath of my winter.

Eyes of Spring

As I gaze into eyes of Spring,
I see your face, little one…
tender wisdom,
strength, and fresh hope.

Again and again,
Spring shows her face,
claims Her place,
flaring with astonishing abundance,
nothing deterring enchanting splendor,
oblivious anything should hold Her back.

Again and again,
you show your face,
claim your place,
like tender crocus up through snow
or pansies not knowing it is still winter,
eager and raring to go with vibrant new life.

Ah,… and as for me,
face now etched by many Springs,
my old eyes anticipate marveling rarity
of each magnificent new creation,
claiming
I, too, may evince such abandon.

Little one,
let's watch Spring's age-old sage,
preparing to splash Her artistry
with playful, exquisite wildness,
unwaveringly,
thrilled by all that magically appears.

Surely spring joyously welcomes our gaze,
musing that Her gifts are truly our gifts,
tender wisdom,
strength, and fresh hope.

Flight on Heron's Wings

I dream flight on expansive wings,
like joining the sweeping careen
of the great blue heron, keeping
keen eyes on our world's soul.

Dreaming of a far-reaching span
to soar over glistening edges
of ebbing tides lifted by winds
that sweep the world with peace.

I wish to be on heron's wings,
touching heaven and earth afar,
rising, descending, into spaces
of humanity's furthest bounds,

Envisioning an elegant world,
immersed in love, in kindness,
imbued with wise compassion,
as I pray flight on heron's wings.

For the Children

May you always have passion for life
and revere all living things.
May you always be inspired
to bring your unique creative energies into form.
May you always honor your power of choice
and respect the greatness
that resides within you.

May you always be tempted to courageously glimpse
into new depths of your soul,
embrace the magnificence of your bright light,
and not be afraid of your own dark corners,
remembering wisdom of the half moon
teaches the necessity of dark and light,
which is inherent to wholeness.

May you tenderly care for your body,
trust your mind, listen intently to your spirit.
May you understand that you
are the author of your wisdom, your joy and love.
May you live with a peaceful heart
and a healthy discontent to continuously seek,
ever-transcending into your best version of you.

Continue

I pray that you intuit that the world needs you,
your contributions,
your choices,
and your legacy.
I pray that you are confident
that your life matters
and shines forth with inspired purpose.

I pray that whatever or whomever your god is,
or becomes,
there is an unshakable knowing deep in your soul
of a loving Divine Presence in the universe—
or multiverses, for all we know,
that also resides eternally at the core of your being,
caring deeply about you and the flow of your life.

Last, and not least, remember . . .
I will always be with you
as you progressively learn to live in freedom
as your *true Self.*
You will never be alone.
I will always be in tandem, by your side,
in this world and in the next.

Grandchild's Stardust

Shimmering luminosity burst
into scattered fiery fragments.
Mystery gathered stardust
sending forth your ray as
the Sacred transformed light
into a sea of water and love,
breathing essence into you
for your birth into this life.

You came, I caressed you,
gazing with star-struck eyes.
I laid you on my awed heart
and a sea of love for all days
swept into my ardent soul.
There, you gifted an anchor
for my life-long purpose
as your seaworthy sage.

You are air for my breath,
words that I cannot speak,
lyrics for unwritten songs,
joy I cannot even quantify.
You fill me with conviction,
with flourishing hope for

Continue

the evolution of brilliance
only supernovas now bear.

As far as stardust goes—
have I seen luminous stars?
Yes, yet not beheld anything
like radiant beauty that you,
dear grandchild, shine forth
from your own sea of love—
illuminating hope and grace
for a grateful, eager world.

I Want To Know

I want to know
what sustains you
from the inside out
when your gut twists,
rolls and wrenches
from unmistakable taste
of sour injustice,
or when love turns its back,
or when your dad dies.

I really want to know
what gives you hope,
what gives you joy
when all else crumbles
down around your socks,
as if your life were leftovers
disintegrating to crumbs
swept off your table
right before your eyes.

What keeps you from
running for cover,
hiding under the eaves
of your otherwise
good-looking life,
when claps of thunder

Continue

117

or heavy, humid smell
of an impending storm
looms in your bones?

Tell me about what
ignites juicy desire
in your soul once again,
what strikes a flame that
bursts forth your *"Yes!"*
your passionate songs,
blazes with inspiration,
helps you hit high C . . .
with your heart unzipped.

What makes you tilt
your gleaming face and
throw happy hands
up to the radiant sun,
topless and barefoot
even if the neighbors,
your dearest friends,
or perhaps your kids,
think you've turned crazy?

I just want to know.

Joy of Wild Abandon

Where did my
joy of wild abandon go?
When did I lose it?
What was I doing
when it slipped away?

Jubilant recklessness,
tousled, ecstatic liberation,
reaching up for the sky,
twirling in an ocean's wind,
crazy in love with sand
warmed by a sun-kissed day,
pushing between my toes
as I bury myself deeply
into ageless, primal history!

I begin to remember again,
all is part of such wonder.
Even I am one
with outrageous mystery,
one with scampering flight
of streaming sandpipers,
hovering,
in whipping circles
of wandering flight.

Continue

How long must I wait
to again mark my bare feet
in grains, weathered
from high inland rocks
carried by winds, by rivers,
joining creatures of the sea
in brief recordings of time
when all is madly free
with joy of wild abandon?

This rousing thrill I long for,
face beaming to the sky,
feet disappearing into sand,
hands circling, reaching,
perhaps even touching
streaming sandpipers,
hovering,
in whipping circles
of wandering flight.

Have I been adrift from this
joy of wild abandon?
Have I really lost its company?
How can I grasp it, hold it
so it doesn't slip away?

My Child

You, my daughter,
carry in your mind
my spirit of seeking,
in your bones
my spirit of wisdom,
in your heart
my spirit of love.

You
came to me, called
by passion of my soul
longing for more,
further than myself,
in gifting the world
beyond my life.

You
carry me past
my future into yours,
expanding afar
my grandest imagination
with your own
exquisite spirit.

Continue

You
take me with you
into many tomorrows,
transcending into
that ever-continuing
sacred thread of
Wisdom's legacy.

No Thing Left Undone

I shall not fall on my knees
praying to the gods
for forgiveness—
for all I have not lived,
for all I have left undone.

Nor will I beg that this one life
truly mattered—
regardless of blindly chosen paths
or naive voices in my head.
Nor will I offer prayers for things
left incomplete in my hands,
incomplete in my heart.

Rather, I will pray to the gods
to give me one more chance
to serve others passionately,
to clear any misgivings,
to create a legacy of good,
and perhaps die while kissing
their precious, blessed earth.

I shall live each day believing
I will use up my life well,

Continue

leaving no thing left undone,

for me, for you . . .

for this generation or the next.

Radiant Twilight

Do you sometimes feel just like
the lights are going out in your life?
In the meantime, don't you believe
what they say about such darkness
and, don't you dare turn away—
stay, with curious eyes wide open.

See a dawn coming toward you
as strong arms of morning's Aurora
start to roll up the curtain of night—
gently pulling tiny stardust diamonds,
deep azure swathes of silky clouds,
higher over her morning silhouette.

You will see, second by second, that
an eager banner of light reveals itself,
as if fresh, dew-drenched satin sheets
hung drying in the stillness of night
wait to gaily whisk on your horizon
at promised moments roosters crow.

As far-flung adventures of the night
begin to rest, smiling into themselves;
as soft diffused light strikes brilliance,

Continue

can you then believe in your heart
that even on dark moonless nights
an exquisite twilight waits for more?

Time

Time, I ponder—

Hearing the loyal tapping
of the kitchen clock's pendulum
reminds me of my grandparents,
remembering, as a child, my family—
Sunday gatherings around the table,
adults talking about important things.
I ate liverwurst, pickles, salty crackers,
listened to the mantel clock ticking
as I sat on a humble, spindly chair
at my small place in the family circle.

Time, I muse—

Realizing it moves the circle of life;
yes, sometimes imperceptibly,
sometimes minutes feel like a year,
yet a year may feel like a minute.
And, this morning neither matters
as, thankfully, life continues to
pull me into it, holding me near,
giving buttery bits of what to know
while I take snapshots by heart
of a dear life that belongs to me.

Continue

Time, I contemplate—

Seventy years evaporated in thin air;
gone, like the in and out of breath.
I wonder who, and I wonder what,
could certainly need me now.
What tables will I gather around?
Will it be honey with salty crackers
that feed new moments of loving,
of thoughtfully helping others, or
that foster a meek sign of belonging,
as I lend an ear while far clocks tick?

Tending the Fire

Chapter 6

Tending the Flames

A Place

Every woman
and every man,
at any age,
must have a place
where heart has
an opening to stillness.

Whether it simply be
in your mind,
or in a corner of your house,
where there is no thing due,
no schedule to pull you,
no nagging debt owed,
no responsibility known,
nor need to call on trust—
a place
where light of the Other
can shine into you.

Whether it be a meadow,
perhaps in the province
of your imagination,
maybe in a cozy chair,
or wild comfort by the sea,

there…
you are certain to discover,
possibly without words,
a glint of something new,
like a new door
with a shiny knob.

An opening
to the one grand
person, place or thing
that wants you,
that needs you,
that invites you in.

Aging

What is this journey of aging—
this unfamiliar dwelling place?

Is it like a house of loneliness
with quiet, cluttered rooms
where pictures on the walls
reflect loss of family, friends,
and the tattered ledger
in the marred old oak desk
still guards
notes in yellowed margins?
There, where doodled dreams
still remain formless because
there simply is not enough
money in lint-edged pockets
for basic needs, let alone
for pipedreams anymore?

Or,

Is it an extraordinary voyage,
a ship setting sail on new seas
with a key banging in the berth—
there, to open a treasure chest,

its bejeweled latch opening to
the seasoned sage,
with maturity and wisdom,
more time, more freedom,
tending forgotten dreams?
I don't really know as yet.
I've not been this old before,
but I choose to climb aboard
with a keen ear to listening
for the knocking of that key.

Awakening

When you awaken in the morning,
don't moan that the clock shines 5 a.m.,
or begrudge disturbance of the wind with rain
howling through the open window,
or ask what the day can do for you.
Awaken asking,
"What makes me come alive?"
"Where is my passion?"

What arouses your heart even more than
waking to a dance of first light shimmering on water—
or savoring sweet sounds of a grandchild's slumber?
Possibly, your heart stirs considering women
who don't have a safe place to sleep.
Perhaps, it is that a woman can now marry a woman.
Maybe it's that idea deep inside that wants to be seen,
and whispers, *You can do whatever you imagine.*

Allow things that stir you to enter your heart.
Breathe freely.
Feel life flowing through your body,
through your being.
What do you love?
What cause tugs at your heart?

What makes you want to celebrate?
What art needs you?

A wise woman opens her eyes in morning
and invites that which desires to live through her,
steadfastly understanding the same power
Hildegard, Theresa, Jesus,
Buddha and QuanYin used
is also in her.
She passionately welcomes her day
in relationship with, and as a co-creator of, life.

Come to Me

Come to me
in the twilight
of my life.
Remind me of awe,
once again
of things
I cannot know.

Tiny birds come
prattling
at my back door.
What would they say
if they could actually
talk about
their high flights?

Marvelous, this life
that I came to,
stories behind stories
with many loves,
terribly, at times hate,
countless lessons
of forgiveness.

My path turned
from prairie grasslands
to salt prairie grass.
Time changes everything.
I wonder,
How do shorebirds ever
say goodbye?

Elderly Trees

Autumn leaves,

fallen

by ensuing winter,

leave new space,

not frantic emptiness.

They free up

places

on aged, gnarly branches

for new beginnings,

new shapes,

new shades,

to emerge

with ease,

with grace,

that, again and again

in effortless ways,

only

elderly trees

reliably

know how best

to do.

Fanciful Dream

After midnight came a fanciful dream,
after my head melted into the pillow,
after tiredness sank into fleece sheets.

I thought it may have been a mistake—
the dream-maker had inadvertently
entered a wrong body, not to be mine.

More so aware, I then began to see
an iridescent, shimmering stream
arising, bursting forth from within me.

Awakened, I lay stunned, a lavish flow
bursting impromptu from my breasts;
yes, a true miracle had found its way.

I hesitantly touched the succulence.
I pressed fingers to my dry, parted lips;
sweetness, like sugar on my tongue.

It tasted like pure love for all humanity;
it tasted like a promise for peace on earth,
like a gift from the tribunal of cosmic gods.

Continue

My eyes flew open, I frantically threw off
swaddled sheets and red woven blanket,
my breasts shimmering wet in moonlight.

I ripped the buttons from my night shirt,
my hands thrashing in vigorous pulls
and I lay bare, wild-eyed in the night...

Journey of Death

I want to know...
why are you afraid
of death?
Why do you shrink
from its word?
Where is the wisdom
in denying our birthright
to its sacred passage—
a path that must be
as miraculous
as coming here
in the first place?

What do you think
when you see
in your mind's eye
your father's sperm
and mother's ovum
diligently traveling
to create you?
Or more so,
even the spark—
or the thought
of you,
before your beginning?

Continue

What do you think
imagining the journey
you forgot—
from conception to body
growing exponentially
moment by moment
in a dark, warm,
watery womb
where your life
depended on a woman
sharing her heat, blood,
food, water and oxygen?

What do you think
picturing the courage
you mustered,
urged by circumstances
greater than you,
moving through darkness
smaller than you,
pushing into the light,
seizing that first breath
as air filled your lungs,
in this totally
foreign place?

What do you think
when you hear
in your mind's ear
your very first cry…
a cosmic cry,
announcing your arrival
in a life
you could not
have envisioned—
adventures and relationships,
experiences
awaiting your discoveries?

What do you think
when you reflect
on all the ideas,
hopes and dreams,
even quests
that you,
only you,
have manifested
in this world—
all a vacuum
without form
before you were born?

Continue

143

What do you think
when you pause
and reflect
with gratitude
the love and joy,
happiness,
the pain and sorrow,
disappointment
that grant a full
rainbow spectrum
of what it is to be alive
here on earth?

What about this dimension—
an outrageous,
inconceivable place
compared to
your once
simple stardust?
Can you dare believe
death's journey
may invite you again
into absolute magnificence

as Divine light streams
toward you again?

Could it be death is
our supreme experience
of true love
from which
we again dream
an unbelievable dream
of a life
we do not know?
Tell me what you think
while I sit here,
drinking my tea,
wondering.

Invitation

What is springtime
than a perfect invitation
for another new beginning?

Curled from a dark winter nap
in my safe, wooly hibernation,
I uncoil within the warm womb,
stretching my fingers out long,
my knees releasing my belly.

I crawl to the door of spring
with eager eyes squinting
into a stunning slit of light,
like a stiff-necked ray piercing
through a boarded cellar door.

Air of spring floods into me
as thawed droplets liberate
the comfortable, cold hold.
I open my anxious arms wide
as if to hug edges of the world.

Boldly bearing my eager heart,
I welcome springtime's opening.

Gratefully, I kiss Her threshold
then reverently,
I whisper,

Please,
May I come on in...
at least one more time?

Oneness

Sweeping past
the corner of my eye
the heron swooped low
between cliffs and trees
careening over shiny rocks
in the rippling stream,
speckly pebbled faces
poking upwards,
like they were waiting
all afternoon for
her grand arrival
at this very moment.

She swept me
with shushing wind,
pulling breath
right out of my soul;
my heart quickened
with sudden arousal,
hearing throbbing of
an ancient drumbeat
calling me to quicken,
calling me to remember
primordial oneness
with great winged ones.

Autumn leaves
gently clapped—
like the tentative
appreciative applause
after a brilliant
spell-bounding act
as I felt her take me
into warm silver folds,
lifting me from earth,
pressing my ear
into the beating
of her fearless heart.

Reverence

I raise my hands
in reverence
for this, my holy land.

This morning, I awaken early,
listen to the noise in my head,
stretch my stiff body, and
tenderly sooth my shoulder—
it's riling ache reminding me
that bones grow old too;
that honor includes this body.

I cautiously roll over and
gently swing out of my bed;
on with a green wool sweater,
both hands cupping coffee,
like receiving communion at
a green stone altar, a blessing
afore stepping into my world.

I see the lake frozen this morning,
draped in broken glass-like angles,
here, there, across a milky surface;
gears of life coming to a halt

for a selfless cherished respite,
gracefully stopping in pure stillness,
inviting veneration for where I am.

A lone squirrel scampers, fleeing,
body stretched long like an arrow;
my eyes catch an empty spider web
stretched across a low fir branch,
frost crystals tinsel its artistic lines,
early sun breaks through the trees
bringing to light stunning splendor.

And, I raise my hands
in reverence
for this, my holy land.

Silent Surrender

In the depths
of an ancient forest,
it is as if
entering a sanctuary
of the gods
where life review begins—
Her roaring waterfalls
growing louder in my ears,
walls of falling into destiny,
crashing over rocks,
filling my voracious heart,
calling me to become no one,
until I become nothing,
like those glassy bubbles
riding past clefts of trees
on light-shard ripples
of rushing water,
then slowly calming…
suddenly disappearing…
into thin air,
like surrendering my life,
past and present,
into
satisfying

contemplative silence,

yet longing

to know more,

to appreciate more,

to love more,

beyond this bend.

Wisdom

Is it wisdom
that the older I am
the less
I truly know about life?

I trust rhythms and cycles
to occur again and again.
I know that long after I die
there will be summers,
there will be rainy days.

Men will bolt for war,
women will ache for peace,
babies will fuss to be fed,
older ones will wonder
once again like children.

But right now, as I sip
my morning coffee,
I don't know any more
about today's mystery than
this taste, or my intention.

Moments, like wrapped
in ribbons and bows,
unknown twists and turns
that by end of day
lay on the floor unfurled.

Each day I am ever left
with my friend named *musing*,
perhaps torn or stunned,
exhilarated, amused,
or hope best, simply content.

Is it wisdom
that now I understand
more
of what I cannot know?

REFLECTION

Tending the Fire

Poetry is a way of giving the soul voice. It speaks to many hearts other than the one that brought the thoughts, the words and phrases into existence. Many times meaning is symbolic, and sometimes raw and realistic. Nonetheless, interpretation is ultimately the reader's choice. Hopefully, the version that is meaningful to you will live on in some transformative way.

Transformation requires us to alter and expand our thinking and behavior beyond familiar feelings and beliefs that root us in the past. When we allow space to examine our perceptions, change in our life begins to appear. We benefit by cultivating the art of self-reflection to identify behaviors that limit change. Poetry offers a means for expanding meditative self-reflection to benefit our thoughtful process.

As sages, we carve out solitude to quiet our minds in order to envision life in new ways. Contemplative time apart from daily demands helps us in creating space for discovery. When we are in touch with what we want in our lives and what we want to make different, we will surely shift from a typical societal destiny.

My intention in sharing poetic expressions relating to the journey of aging is to create interest in a new vision with a different perspective than convention. I believe this is a time for us to consciously envision our lives in more open-hearted ways. As sage leaders ever deepening in authenticity, passion, compassion, and in creating new visions, we will manifest opportunities for greater personal fulfillment. And, we will influence meaningful changes for greater good in this generation and future generations.

If you have completed reading *Tending the Fire*, no doubt you have a desire to manifest and sustain a meaningful and fulfilling later life. *Awakening Fire in the Heart—Women and the Liberating Journey of Aging* is a companion book that offers further exploration. Life is a sacred journey and we are meant to enjoy that journey with as much liberation as we can create.

May we meet, tending our fires…

Marilyn Loy Every, DMin
Poet of Life

ABOUT THE AUTHOR

Tending the Fire

Dr. Marilyn Loy Every holds a Doctor of Ministry in Wisdom Studies, with a focus on aging, and Certification in Spiritual Direction from Ubiquity University, San Francisco, California. She also holds a Master of Arts in Counseling Psychology from St. Martin's College in Olympia, Washington, a Master of Science in Audiology from the University of Wyoming, and a Bachelor of Science from the University of Nebraska. Dr. Loy Every is also a Certified Sage-ing Leader with Sage-ing International. She specializes in aging issues, sage leadership training, affirmative aging guidance, life visioning, and spiritual companioning.

Marilyn Loy Every is the visionary and founder of Sagessence, LLC, a company with a mission to develop and facilitate programs that inspire and prepare women and men to re-envision aging in the second half of their lives. She is passionate about promoting affirmative transformation of personal and cultural views that honor aging in our society so we may complete our lives with a most magnificent sense of meaningful fulfillment. Her belief is that in learning new possibilities in aging, embracing liberating images, and honoring change, we can more fully contribute to our communities and to the wellbeing of future generations.

Dr. Loy Every is also author of *Awakening Fire in the Heart— Women and the Liberating Journey of Aging*, and *Fire in the Well— Poetry for Women Awakening the Inner Sage*. She continues to inspire women, as well as men, in the second half of life in creating the life they love.

Visit the Sagessence website at www.sagessence.com.